Python Version 3.2 Introduction using IDLE and PythonWin

For Linux-Debian and Microsoft Windows
First Edition

Herb Norbom

Author of:
Robot Wireless Control Made Simple with Python and C
Python Version 2.6 Introduction using IDLE
Python Version 2.7 Introduction using IDLE

Where we are aware of a trademark that name has been printed with a Capital Letter.

Great care has been taken to provide accurate information, by both the author and the publisher, no expressed or implied warranty of any kind is given. No liability is assumed for any damages in connection with any information provided.

Table of Contents

Note, in the Table of Contents lines beginning with a # are program names.

PREFACE

Congratulations on selecting Python. While I am sure everyone has their own favorite programming language and good reasons for it, at this point Python is my choice. As you learn Python you will gain insight into areas you are going to need to write programs in other modern languages. There are several reasons for choosing Python, they include the following:

- Object Oriented – will flow with events rather than straight lines
- Not compiled, uses an interpreter – therefore, quick results while developing applications
- Runs on Windows, Linux, Unix, even Apple – it is portable
- There is lot of FREE information on the web about it
- Python is free
- There are a lot of free modules - you will need –for communication, etc.
- What you learn, program flow and structure will to some extent carry over to C, C++ or C#, or whatever language you evolve to
- Python is a dynamic language that continues to thrive with new features.

Yes, of course there are disadvantages, if you are going to do something for resale Python may not be the language for you. If you are here, you are probably not close to having anything to sell, so don't worry about that. Just because Python uses an interpreter do not think you are limited in terms of program size and complexity. With today's computer's Python will be fast enough for you. So I wore you down, now you may be wondering, where can I get Python and how hard will it be to install? You are in luck, I will give you the sites and it is not hard to install. Keep in mind that many operating systems come with Python installed; some will even have two versions. Check out your computer prior to going through the download effort. This book is based on Python 3.2, look for my other books if you already have a different Python version.

When you are looking at Python version the first number is the most significant. For example you would have a hard time finding the difference between Python 2.6.6 and Python 2.6.8. But the difference between

Python 2.7.5 and Python 3.3.2 is quite significant.

FORWARD

The purpose of this book is to provide a quick introduction to Python. The reader is introduced to Python version 3.2. A feature for the Windows version is PythonWin. At this point it is only available for Windows, and if you are using Windows you will want to use this great new feature. We will also use Python's standard editor and shell programs, named IDLE. The book also provides instructions on running Python under PC Windows and PC Linux environments. As I write the book I will test all Python 3.2.3 programs on Linux-Debian and on the PC-Microsoft Windows® using Python 3.2.2 from ActiveState. Program screen shots will be based on the PC window. Where there are differences to the Linux-Debian environment I will note them.

My goal is to provide a description area for what the program is going to do, show the program and then the Python Shell for the output.

GETTING STARTED

Of course you need to have Python on your system. Many computers in the Linux/Unix world have Python installed. I will be using two computers for all the examples.
PC – Microsoft Windows® XP with service pack 3 installed has the following Python version:
       Python 3.2.2.3   from ActiveState Software Inc. the community edition
To see if Python is installed on a Windows machine click on Start\All Programs and see if any Python items are listed.

Linux-Debian 7.0 Raspberry "wheezy" :
       Python 3.2.3   installed with Linux-Debian

Important note for Linux/Unix computers. Python is generally installed with the operating system. I would HIGHLY recommend that you NOT install a newer Python version unless you are very clear as to just what Python is used for on your system. A simple method to see if Python is installed is to go to a command or terminal prompt and type "python". If Python is installed you will see the version. To exit Python command prompt '>>>' press Ctrl + z key. If for some reason Python is not installed I would suggest you check Synaptic Package Manager or Aptitude.

Of course you only need one version of Python on your computer.
       http://www.python.org/getit/ This site has a good list of versions and the downloads.

Two other sites that you can obtain the software from.
       www.activestate.com   The community Edition is FREE.
       www.sourceforge.net
All three sites are very good, you will have choices as to versions, etc. You can get the binary files and avoid having to compile. All the sites have good download tools and instructions. There can be differences in which versions a site offers.

PYTHON SHELL and TEXT EDITOR

You have many choices including Python's standard editor 'IDLE' which is installed with the Windows versions. For Linux you will probably need to install 'IDLE' using synaptic, aptitude or apt-get. The programs shown will be developed using IDLE. There are many advantages to using IDLE over other text editors. The biggest is probably that it is installed automatically on Windows environments.(see Linux-Debian for instructions on that environment). While there are many other advantages consider the HELP function for accessing your version's Python Documentation.

Linux-Debian installation of IDLE-python

On the Raspberry-Pi idle-python3.2.3 was installed along with Python automatically. If you need to find the executable it was installed as usr/bin/idle-python3.2 and/or usr/bin/idle3.

With the Raspberry LXDE GUI to add an item to desktop. You can use the editor that is available on your system to make a file. Save the file, adjusted as appropriate for your system, as shown below to your desktop folder. I saved my file with the name "idle.desktop".

```
[Desktop Entry]
Name=IDLE3
Comment=Integrated Development Environment for Python3
Exec=/usr/bin/idle3
Icon=/usr/share/pixmaps/idle3.xpm
Terminal=false
MultipleArgs=false
Type=Application
Categories=Application;Development;
StartupNotify=true
```

In Linux-Debian if you are using the Gnome GUI. To add an icon to the desktop, right click on a blank area of the screen and select 'Create Launcher'. Your Type will be 'Application', Name as you like, Command in my case is '/usr/bin/idle-python3.2'.

IDLE-Python Shell

Let us make sure that IDLE and Python are working. We will use IDLE and the Python Shell to write and run our first program. The Python Shell looks pretty much the same for all versions. On different versions when you execute IDLE one of two windows may open. If the Python Shell opens that is fine for this purpose. If an Untitled window is what opened, click on Run and select Python Shell. Our first program will be very simple, we just want to make sure everything is working and you can check what version of Python you are running.

If you want to set defaults for which Window to open do the following. Under either Window (Edit Window or Shell Window) you can select Options/Configure IDLE/General and set the defaults for which window to open along with other options. (Sorry you can only choose one window as default to open.) There are various settings, I suggest you leave them as they are for now, but as you get more confident change them as you desire.

Our first program is the traditional 'Hello World'. You will note that we assign the string "Hello World" to a variable named 'greeting'. In Python you do not need to assign data types, it is done automatically. A string must be enclosed in " " or ' '.

As you work on this program in the Python Shell you may note that is somewhat interactive and running, as you complete typing a command and press return, the command runs. We want to print our variable 'greeting' on the Python Shell.

Starting IDLE

Start the IDLE program. (Windows example under Start\AllPrograms\Python3.2\IDLE(Python GUI). You will probably want to create a short-cut. Right click on IDLE(Python GUI) and select create short-cut. Grab the new short-cut and slide to your desktop.

Linux-Debian from desktop if you added an icon, otherwise look under usr/bin/idle-python3.2 for example. From the terminal type "idle-python3.2" or from a File Browser double left click and in my case select "Execute" or "Run" to open the Python Shell.

Our traditional greeting and as you see our first error. In Python 3.x the print statement has been changed to a function. Many of the old print statements will work if you enclose the items to be printed within ( ). Note in the following example the old statement 'print greeting' generates an error. But, when the item to be printed is enclosed in the ( ) the new function executes. Many of the changes incorporated into Python 3.0 were back-ported to Python 2.7.

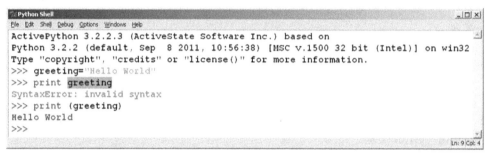

PYTHON IDLE MENU ITEMS

Under 'File' you have the usual items of New Window, open, recent files, and etc. You also have two items that may be new to you. Some other useful menu selections are also shown. There are of course other items that you can explore.

Class Browser

This will get more useful as your programs get more complicated. In the simplest terms a program is a 'Class'. So if you click on it after you have saved a program it will just list the current program. But later we will define a 'Class'. This feature will list the Classes defined in the program.

Path Browser

This is useful in showing you the search paths that Python uses under sys.path. As you add third party packages of particular use will be the Python\32\lib\site-packages.

Edit\Go to Line

You need to open a New Window and save a file before this feature can be used. When you enter a line number your cursor jumps to that line. I can see using this when you have a program error and you want to go to the line that had the error. Other than that it would be nice if line numbers were listed in the editor.

Format\Comment Out_Region

You need to open a New Window and save a file before this feature can be used. This is a nice feature for commenting out sections or blocks of code. Highlight the line you want to comment out and select this item.

Use the same technique to remove the commenting out, only choose 'Uncomment Region'.

Help\Python Docs

This is very useful, saves a lot of time in particular because the feature is specific for your version of Python.

Python Text Editor

This is where you will spend most of your time developing programs. With the text editor you can save your programs and easily run them. You need to have an Untitled Window open at this point, from within IDLE. If only the Python Shell is open, click on File and select New Window. We will repeat our greeting with slight modifications. We will add a comment line. In Python anything after the '#' is considered to be a comment. We are going to need to understand Python modules, so let us import one to get started. We will import 'sys' which has a lot of useful traits. We will just touch on a couple to give you an idea. Try using the Help item and check 'sys' out in the Python Documentation under Global Module Index.

Generally you will want your import statements first in the program, just makes it easier, as long as the module is imported before you reference the function the program will work.

You may note that in assigning values to the variable pyVersion I added a description and a '+' sign to include our sys.version information. The '+' sign is a great way to combine or concatenate strings. For all of our examples I will include the Python Version as a comment in the program to help differentiate the version examples, this I find very helpful when looking at other peoples programs.

Save your program by clicking on File/Save. Set up a directory where you can easily find and backup your work. Your program file-name must have the py extension. For example: 'Hello.py'. The system will make you save the file prior to running the program.

Run your program by clicking Run and Run Module. We will be writing our code or script or program in the Window Editor the output will be displayed in the Python Shell.

```
#Hello.py
#this is a comment, everything after the # is a comment
#Python 3.2.2  RyMax, Inc.  8/1/2013
greeting="Hello Again, World"
print (greeting)
print () # just add a blank line to output
print ()
#import the sys module
import sys
#check the Python version info
pyVersion="PythonVersion= "+sys.version
print (pyVersion)
```

```
7% Python Shell                                                    _ □ x
File  Edit  Shell  Debug  Options  Windows  Help
>>> ====================== RESTART ======================
>>>
Hello Again, World


PythonVersion= 3.2.2 (default, Sep  8 2011, 10:56:38) [MSC v.1500
32 bit (Intel)]
>>> |
                                                              Ln: 492 Col: 4
```

If you had problems with this it maybe related to the 'case'. Python is 'case' sensitive; pyVersion and pyversion are two separate variables.

PythonWin

As mentioned earlier this is a feature available only on Windows versions. This has some very nice features and it has retained the key ingredients of IDLE. If you are working on Windows you will want to get the Windows Extensions for Python. I believe the ActiveState Community version includes this set, or at least part of it. If not available on your Windows systems search either SourceForge or Python .org.

This is only available for Windows, sorry Linux-Debian users. To be able to use it you will probability need to download and install Python for Windows extensions. There are a number of features that if you plan on developing applications for Windows that you will want. Check out the sites mentioned earlier for information on the extensions.

To start PythonWin go to Start\AllPrograms\Python3.2\PythonWin. You will probably want to create a short-cut. Right click on PythonWin and select create short-cut. Grab the new short-cut and slide to your desktop. The executable is installed under C:\Python32\Lib\site-packages\pythonwin on my system. Your initial window that opens contains a Window named PythonWin (I guess it is the main control) and an Interactive Window (like the Python Shell). You can run programs from the Interactive Window just as we did before.

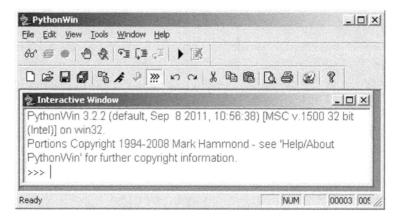

To use as a text editor click on File\New\Python Script and you will see a somewhat familiar screen that works as your text editor. One new feature that I really like is that you can now have line numbers. To turn this feature on in the PythonWin Window select View\Options\Editor. Increase the Margin Widths for Line

Numbers to at least ten. Then when you open a new script you will have line numbers. I have shown in the following a test script that has an error. When I selected File\Run\No debugging you can note the error is shown at the bottom of the window. I think the PythonWin is a very fine addition.

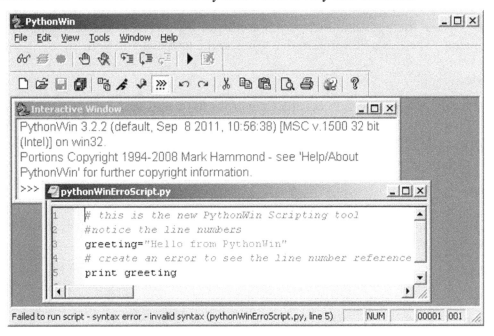

To correct the error change line 5 to "print (greeting)", just add the brackets. From this point on I will be using IDLE and showing the programs as text vs screen shots. For the programs I have added comments for the start and end of the program to help distinguish the programs from regular text. The output I will also show as text with the heading 'PYTHON SHELL'.

WORKING WITH DATA TYPES
In Python you do not need to define a type to your variables. Python automatically handles this and it is important to note that within a program a variables data type can be changed just by assigning data of a different type. In the next examples we are going to work with the standard data types: Bool, Number, String and Tuple.

Operators

OPERATOR	MEANING	EXAMPLE	RESULT
+	addition	3 + 4	7
-	subtraction	4 – 3	1
/	division	4.00 / 2.00	2.0
*	multiplication	4*2	8
**	exponentiation	4**2	16
<	less than	3 is less than 4, use in if statement, if (3<4):	TRUE
<=	less than or equal	3 is less than or equal to 4, use in if statement, if(3<=4):	TRUE
>	greater than	4 greater than 3, use in if statement, if(3>4):	FALSE
>=	greater than or equal	4 greater than or equal to 3, use in if statement, if(3>=4):	FALSE
==	equal to	4 equal to 4, use in if statement, if(4==4):	TRUE
!=	not equal	4 not equal to 4, use in if statement, if (4!=4):	FALSE

There are other operators for example bit manipulation that are not displayed.

Your algebra days have caught up with you. These are the main Operator's that we will be concerned with. You may see others that do the same thing, some of those are from prior versions of Python, even though they may work. I recommend you use these. In the Python documentation you will find items referred to as 'depreciated'. For Python 'depreciated' means you are being warned of future non-support. You can use it, but it is on the way out. There is a newer item that you should start using in your code.

Order of Operations

When working with numbers you need to consider the order of operations. Python uses the standard order of operations that you may have learned in algebra. Do you remember the mnemonic PEMDAS?
Please Excuse My Dear Aunt Sally.

	Order of Operations	Python Syntax
P	Parentheses	(…)
E	Exponents	**
M	Multiplication	*
D	Division	/
A	Addition	+
S	Subtraction	-

Remember with Parentheses you work from the inside out.

Bool

Bool variables have only two possible values, True and False. Many of the built in functions that do some sort of testing return a yes/no response. Meaning there is a True or False type response. 'True' could be a '1' and 'False' could be a '0'. There are other values as well. Let us start with 'False' first. False can be represented by None, False, 0, 0.0, '', (), [], {}, (basically any value that starts with a '0' or an empty value).

True is practically anything else, for example: 'True' is any non-zero value. Examples: Yes, 1, 11111111, myname, (23), True, etc.

Number Types

Number Types are int, long, float, and complex, and are basically the same in most computer languages. One of the most frustrating things in technical descriptions is that they always seem to refer to another technical description. For example the difference between 'int' and 'long' is the precision. I am glad we cleared that up for you. In Python, unless you are well into developing big numbers you do not care, Python is handling it for you. So I am going to skip over 'precision' until we need it. Float deals with the decimal point and the precision (positions to the right of the point). A complex number, we will not use other than maybe in as example is a number that has real and imaginary components. If you need more information there is a bunch on the web.

Working With Numbers, Boolean and Float

In our next program we will work with numbers, boolean and float examples. I suggest you enter the program in sections, save and run. Once you are comfortable with a section add the next one. You will note in many of the examples, particularly where we are testing if one value is equal to another, that we use two equal signs together. We use two of the equal signs because we want to compare and not assign a value. In many of the examples the two equals signs show as two horizontal lines and you may not initially recognize that it is two equal signs "=="back to back..

DataTypes.py   simple manipulation

```python
#START PROGRAM
# using Python 3.2.2
# author Herb  8/2/2013 RyMax, Inc.

# using numbers
x=5
y=6
z=(x+y)*5                        #addition and multiplication
print ("z= ",z)


zz=z/2                          # division
print ("zz= ",zz)


zzz=(2*(x+y))*z                 #addition,nested paranthese, multiplication
print ("zzz= ",zzz)


zzzz= x**2                      # exponent
print ("zzzz= ",zzzz)


# Boolean
x =2
y =5
boolzz = x<y                    # boolean less than
print ("boolzz= ",boolzz)


x = 5
boolzz = x!=y                   #boolean not equal to
print ("boolzz= ", boolzz)
if boolzz == 0:
        print ("boolzz is equal to 0 and False")


boolzz = x==y                   #boolean equal to
print ("boolzz= ", boolzz)

if boolzz == 1:
        print ("boolzz is equal to 1 and True")


#some float examples
x=5
y=5.5
z= x+y                          #float addition
print ("z as a float addition= ", z)


z= x/y
print ("z as a float division= ", z)
#END OF PROGRAM
```

```
PYTHON SHELL
>>> ===================== RESTART =====================
>>>
z= 55
zz= 27
zzz= 1210
zzzz= 25
boolzz= True
boolzz= False
boolzz is equal to 0 and False
boolzz= True
boolzz is equal to 1 and True
z as a float addition= 10.5
z as a float division= 0.909090909091
>>>
```

Working With Strings

Python Strings are just about any character or number contained within quotation marks, either " " or ' '. In this example we will expand on our initial string variable 'greeting' and add more manipulation of the string variables. As we saw earlier Python is case sensitive. With strings and numbers there are differences in how they are typed. For example the number 1 and the string "1" are very different. With Python we can convert the integer type to string and back again with ease. There are many 'methods' available for working with strings. In the following example I will show a number of them. We are also introducing the concept of passing data to a function or method. The value or variable contained within the ( ) of a function is passed to the function. Remember 'print' is now a function. When the function completes it returns the value and in our case we assign the returned value to a different variable when we are striping leading spaces from a string as shown in the following.

strings.py

```python
#START PROGRAM
# using Python 3.2.2
# author Herb  8/2/2013 RyMax, Inc.

#The basic string is just text assigned to a variable,
# or plain text enclosed in " "  or ' '

x="     This is so much fun"  #assign the text & spaces to the variable
print (x)

y =" and I sure hope we get a lot of homework!"
print (y)
z = ' still more text'
print (z)
print (x + y + z)
print ()
print ()

#String Methods
print (x)
xstrip= str.lstrip(x)          #take off the leading spaces
```

```
print (xstrip)

xSwapCase= str.swapcase(x)      #change all lower case to upper
print (xSwapCase)               #and all upper to lower case

xlower = str.lower(xSwapCase)   #change all to lower case
print (xlower)

xUPPER = str.upper(xlower)
print (xUPPER)

#END OF PROGRAM
```

PYTHON SHELL
```
>>> ===================== RESTART =====================
>>>
    This is so much fun
 and I sure hope we get a lot of homework!
 still more text
    This is so much fun and I sure hope we get a lot of homework! still more text


    This is so much fun
This is so much fun
    tHIS IS SO MUCH FUN
    this is so much fun
    THIS IS SO MUCH FUN
>>>
```

Tuple's

Tuple's are an extremely useful data type because you can mix data types within a tuple. Once the data type is assigned within the tuple you cannot change the data type. Once you have mastered the tuple you will wish all programming languages had the capability.   A tuple is similar to a list or an array. In a tuple you can change the individual data values but not the individual data types. Once you have a handle on some of the rules, tuple's will be a good data tool. You define a tuple using ( ) with the last tuple data item followed by a comma. The best way to explain tuple's is through an example.

tuples.py

```
#START PROGRAM
# using Python3.2.2
# author Herb  8/2/2013 RyMax, Inc.

x=()            # define an empty tuple
x1=('one',)     # define a tuple with just one value

y=('Herb', 'this', 'is',99,'percent','mud',)

print ("All the values of the tuple y: ",y)

print ("Just the third value of y: ", y[3])
# you may have expected to see 'is' printed
```

```
# but a tuple is similar to an array,
# the first variable is 0, so '99' is in position 3

z=('Fred', 'is','smart',)

#moving portions of two tuples to a new tuple
#you can not delete values, but you do not have to move them

newT=z[0]+y[2]+'88'+y[4]+z[2]
print (newT)
#play with this, add some spaces between the words

#you can easily combine two tuples
combT = y+z
print (combT)

#END OF PROGRAM
```

```
PYTHON SHELL
>>> ===================== RESTART =====================
>>>
All the values of the tuple y:  ('Herb', 'this', 'is', 99, 'percent', 'mud')
Just the third value of y:  99
Fredis88percentsmart
('Herb', 'this', 'is', 99, 'percent', 'mud', 'Fred', 'is', 'smart')
>>>
```

Determining Data Types

Remember the integer 1 and the string "1" are very different. With Python we can covert the integer type to string or text and back again with ease, the hard part is remembering what you are working with. Sometimes we need to use methods to determine what our variable type is and then decide how to proceed. Our next program works with some of the issues. Note in the program that the same variable changes from 'int' to 'str' type.   With changing types being so easy it is great that Python has tests to determine the variable types.

If you are going from string to integer you should use the error catching techniques we will discuss later. For that matter anytime you can have an uncertain result it is good technique to use error catching, within reasonable limits of course.

 # whatistype.py   what is our data type?

```
#START PROGRAM
# using Python3.2.2
# author Herb  8/2/2013 RyMax, Inc.

x = 5
y = 4.55
z="my test string"

# identify what types we have
print ("x=5 is type: ",type(x))
print ("y=4.555 is type: ",type(y))
```

```python
print ("z=my test string is type: ",type(z))

# based on the type let's make some logic decisions and change the type

# Look at x, if we test it and find it to be an integer we will
#change it to be a string

intType = type(x) is int
print (intType)

if intType ==True:
        print ("yes it is an integer")
        x = str(x)        #change to string
strType = type(x) is int
print ("test x to see if still an int type: ",strType)

strType = type(x) is str
print ("test x to see if changed to string type: ",strType)

#END OF PROGRAM
```

```
>>> ===================== RESTART =======================
>>>
x=5 is type:  <class 'int'>
y=4.555 is type:  <class 'float'>
z=my test string is type:  <class 'str'>
True
yes it is an integer
test x to see if still an int type:  False
test x to see if changed to string type:  True
>>>
```

OUTPUT FORMATING

Using the % Method

As our skills have grown our ability to produce 'nice' formatted output has not grown to any extent. We are going to spend a little time formatting output. This gets a little cryptic, but Python is logical, once you get the hang of what it is trying to do. A little description may help. Remember Print is a function, enclose everything in ( ). As before our text to print is enclosed in " ". The formatting control symbol is '%' and that symbol is placed within the text " " where we want to print our variable data to print. Once we close the " we then place another '%' and our variable. The actual formatting is done immediately after the first % within the text. Much easier to see in the following example.

outputFormatting.py   formatting our output using %

```python
#START PROGRAM
# using Python3.2.2
# author Herb  8/2/2013 RyMax, Inc.

# for formatting strings the '%' starts the definition
```

```
x=1033.3423542424
print ("the value of x is: ",x)            #no formatting

#limit the value of x to 3 decimal places
print ("the value of x is: %1.3f"%x)

#limit the value of x to 3 decimal places
print ("the value of x is: %3.3f"%x)

#limit the value of x to 5 decimal places
print ("the value of x is: %3.5f"%x)
print ("the value of x is: %+3.5f"%x)
print ("the value of x is: %3.2f%%"%x)


y=-9.8437202
print ( )
print ("the value of y is: ",y)
print ("the value of y is: %3.3f "%y)


#print "%s this is total %1.3f %s and a percent of %3.2f%%"%x %x
yy= .75
text1='this is total'
text2='and a percent of '

print ("%s %1.3f %s %3.2f%%"%(text1,x, text2,yy))

#END OF PROGRAM

PYTHON SHELL
>>> ===================== RESTART =====================
>>>
the value of x is:  1033.34235424
the value of x is: 1033.342
the value of x is: 1033.342
the value of x is: 1033.34235
the value of x is: +1033.34235
the value of x is: 1033.34%

the value of y is:  -9.8437202
the value of y is: -9.844
this is total 1033.342 and a percent of  0.75%
>>>
```

Using Format Method

Format our output using the newer format class. This became standard in Python 2.6, and I would expect it to be the dominant format option in the future. As you work through the example think how to enhance it, add a tuple, and work on formatting that output. With the format class you can also format dates, right justify, and it has many more features.

 # outputFormattingNew.py   *the new formatting method*

```python
##START PROGRAM
# using Python3.2.2
# author Herb  8/2/2013 RyMax, Inc.


x=1033.3423542424
#no format
print ("the entire value of x is "+format(x))

#limit the value of x to 3 decimal places
print ('the value of x without sign and only 3 decimals: '+ "{0:.3f}".format(x))

#limit the value of x to 5 decimal places
print ('the value of x with sign and only 5 decimals: '+ "{0:+.5f}".format(x))
y=-9.8437202
print ('the value of y with sign and only 3 decimals: '+ "{0:+.3f}".format(y))

# compound statements
yy= .75
text1='this is total '
text2=' and a percent of '
print ("{0:s}""{1:.3f}""{2:s}""{3:.2%}".format(text1,x, text2, yy))



#lining up columns
x=100
y=10
z=2000
name='Herb'
name2='Raymond'
print (name, x, y ,z)
print (name2, y, z ,x)
print
print ("Now using the format line")
#format to get it aligned
#looking at {0:10} we are saying print variable 0 which is 'name'
#and the 'name' will use 10 spaces and be left justified, the default
print ("{0:10}""{1:8}""{2:5}""{3:6}".format(name, x, y, z))
print ("{0:10}""{1:8}""{2:5}""{3:6}".format(name2, y, z, x))

#format 'name' centered in the 10 positions
print ("{0:^10}""{1:8}""{2:5}""{3:6}".format(name, x, y, z))

#include a string description with the formated number, note the + sign
print ("This is z=2000  {0:+4}".format(z))

yy=-9.8437202
#include a string description with the formated number, note the - sign
print ("This is yy=-9.8437202 {0:-.4f}".format(yy))
```

```
#add a size to the above
print ("This is yy=-9.8437202 {0:-12.4f}".format(yy))
#add limit to three decimals and see if rounds or truncate
print ("This is yy=-9.8437202 {0:-12.3f}".format(yy))


#END OF PROGRAM
```

```
>>> ====================== RESTART ======================
>>>
the entire value of x is 1033.3423542424
the value of x with out sign and only 3 decimals: 1033.342
the value of x with sign and only 5 decimals: +1033.34235
the value of y with sign and only 3 decimals: -9.844
this is total 1033.342 and a percent of 75.00%
Herb 100 10 2000
Raymond 10 2000 100
Now using the format line
Herb        100  10 2000
Raymond      10 2000  100
   Herb     100  10 2000
This is z=2000 +2000
This is yy=-9.8437202 -9.8437
This is yy=-9.8437202     -9.8437
This is yy=-9.8437202     -9.844
>>>
```

There are alignment options, note in the last line of the program the use of the '^' or hat symbol. This indicates to place the text in the center of the defined field size. Some other options are listed in the following. The last examples in the program used several of the Options shown in the table.

Option	Meaning
<	Left align within available space, default for most objects
>	Right align within available space, default for numbers
=	For numbers only to force padding after the sign if any
^	Center the object to be centered within available space
	If a field size is not defined, the field width will be same size as the object
+	Include sign for positive and negative numbers
-	Include sign for negative numbers only
space	put a space in front of positive numbers and a minus sign in front of negative numbers

PROGRAM INPUTS

We are going to build one program that prompts for input from the console and displays your input back on the console. Next we are going to go through various examples for reading and writing text files. I suggest you enter the code in sections. The complete code will be shown at the end along with all the Python Shell output.

The console input is very easy to use with Python. We are going to use a built_in function. The raw_input function has been discontinued. In place use just 'input( )' as shown in the example, this always returns a string and strips off the newline controls. Use the string to integer conversions shown earlier if you need the input to be an integer. The prompt string will be shown on the console or your standard output. Note we save the user's input to the variable 'nameEntered'.

Using Input

```
# simpleInput.py   begin exploring methods of loading data
# using Python3.2.2
# author Herb  8/2/2013 RyMax, Inc.

#SECTION1
# will generate prompt on console, press enter when done
nameEntered= input("Enter your name: ")
print ("Hi "+ nameEntered)
```

Save and run the above code.

File-Input

The file input is also very easy to use. There are a lot of options. For now we will consider opening, reading, writing and closing the file. One of the most basic is the Built-in Function 'open'. It is worthwhile getting to know the Built-In Functions as you do not need to import modules. You of course need to include a file name. The file name will be the first argument in the open function. When you open a file you need to be aware of the 'mode'. The 'mode' is a string that gives instruction on how to open the file, it is the second argument. For example 'r' is read only. The default is 'r' so you can omit it if you desire, but I suggest you always include the 'mode' as a point of clarification for your code. The mode values are shown below. Check the Python documentation for more detailed information. When you open or write to a file there is a high probability for an error to occur. We will consider error handling a little later.

MODE	Description
r	read only (this is default)
w	write, creates a new file, if the file exits it is erased first (in effect empties file)
a	write and append to file (usually to end of file)
r+	opens file for both reading and writing
t	text mode(this is the default)
	WINDOWS and Linux can also have a binary mode but there are differences, read the documentation
rb	read binary
wb	write binary
r+b	read and write binary

As we start working with files I have created two text files using the IDLE editor. Remember to save the files in your current program directory and to use a .txt extension.

FIRST TXT FILE,   named   simpleTextfile.txt
First, Second, Third, John, Fred

SECOND TXT FILE, named   lineTextfile.txt
First
Second
Third
John
Fred

In the code shown in the following a number of features have been added. I suggest you continue entering the code in sections. In SECTION2 we open the file using the basic 'open' statement. Notice the file name and the mode included in the open statement. We also read the entire file into the variable 'entirefile' and then print the contents. You need to be aware of system memory and buffer size when reading an entire file. Our final statement is to close the file.

```
#SECTION2
#a simple file read and print to console, using this
#method you must close the file
f= open('simpleTextfile.txt', 'r')
entirefile=f.read()
print ('This is entire file using a simple open')
print (entirefile)
f.close()
```

In the code SECTION3 we read in only two lines of our second text file. We use the readline() function which gives you more control of your data with less work.. We only print the first two lines in the example. A quick introduction to the 'if statement'. We enclose the argument to test in ( ). A colon is added at the end of the line. If the tested condition is true, the indented lines following the test are executed. All lines that are indented are executed. End the indenting to end the 'if statement '. IDLE has tab settings which are fine to use for the indents. If you desire to use the space-bar that is fine also. Just be aware that Python is very sensitive to spacing. If the indents or the spacing is not the same Python will give an error.

```
#SECTION3
#another simple file read, note datafile organized differently
#remember to close your file
workfile="lineTextfile.txt"
f=open(workfile, 'r')
print ("first line of lineTextfile")
firstline=f.readline()
print (firstline)
if (firstline !="):
    secondline=f.readline()
    print ("the second line of lineTextfile= " + secondline)
f.close()
```

In our next section we use the 'with open' statement. It works the same as the 'open statement' with an important difference, it automatically closes the file. I omitted the mode, as you can see it opens in the default mode of 'read'. Notice the use of indents.

```
#SECTION4
#Using a different method to open file, note this automatically
#closes the file when finished reading it
print ("This is SECTION4 data from simpleTextfile using 'with open'")
with open('simpleTextfile.txt') as f:
    for data in f:
        print (data)
```

Next we use a variable name for the filename. Using our file defined in the third section of the program.
```
#SECTION5
#Using same method on different file structure
print ("This is SECTION5 data from lineTextfile using 'with open'")
with open(workfile) as f:
    for data in f:
        print (data)
```

In our next section we turn off the automatic line feed of the print statement. Notice the use of the comma in the print statement.
```
#SECTION6
```

```
#Using same method but avoiding automatic line feed after print
# You can strip off the line feed or as below turn off the automatic
#linefeed by using the end qualifier
print 'This is SECTION6 data from lineTextfile with automatic line feed off'
with open(workfile) as f:
    for data in f:
        print (data, end="")
```

In SECTION7 we create a file named 'testWriteFile. The mode 'a' is used which creates a file if it doesn't exist or appends the data to the end if it does exist.

```
#SECTION7
#this will create file if it does not exist,
#if the file exists will append data to it
#run the program several times and you will see data appended to file
#you can use IDLE to examine the file, Click File\Open find the file
#you will probably want more control
with open('testWriteFile.txt','a') as f:
    f.write("more new stuf")
```

Continuing with our write example, you may have thought the output was not what you wanted. In the string to be written a '\n' is added at the beginning of the string. In Python a '\' can be viewed as an escape character and it is telling the program that what immediately follows is to be treated as a command or instruction. In our case we put an 'n' to indicate we wanted a new line prior to writing the data to the file.

```
#SECTION8
#let us do another append to the file, this time
    #we will append data on a new line
with open('testWriteFile.txt','a') as f:
    f.write("\nmore new stuff")
```

The complete program is shown next.

 # simpleInput.py   begin exploring methods of loading data

```
#START PROGRAM
# using Python3.2.2
# author Herb  8/2/2013 RyMax, Inc.

#SECTION1
# will generate prompt on console, press enter when done
nameEntered= input("Enter your name: ")
print ("Hi "+ nameEntered)

#SECTION2
#a simple file read and print (to console, using this
#method you must close the file
f= open('simpleTextfile.txt', 'r')
entirefile=f.read()
print ('This is entire file using a simple open')
print (entirefile)
f.close()

#SECTION3
#another simple file read, note datafile organized differently
```

```python
#remember to close your file
workfile="lineTextfile.txt"
f=open(workfile, 'r')
print ("first line of lineTextfile")
firstline=f.readline()
print (firstline)
if (firstline !=''):
    secondline=f.readline()
    print ("the second line of lineTextfile= " + secondline)
f.close()


#SECTION4
#Using a different method to open file, note this automatically
#closes the file when finished reading it
print ("This is SECTION4 data from simpleTextfile using 'with open'")
with open('simpleTextfile.txt') as f:
    for data in f:
        print (data)


#SECTION5
#Using same method on different file structure
print ("This is SECTION5 data from lineTextfile using 'with open'")
with open(workfile) as f:
    for data in f:
        print (data)


#SECTION6
#Using same method but avoiding automatic line feed after print
# You can strip off the line feed or as below turn off the automatic
#linefeed by using the end qualifier
print ('This is SECTION6 data from lineTextfile with automatic line feed off')
with open(workfile) as f:
    for data in f:
        print (data, end="")


#SECTION7
#this will create file if it does not exist,
#if the file exists will append data to it
#run the program several times and you will see data appended to file
#you can use IDLE to examine the file, Click File\Open find the file
#you will probably want more control
with open('testWriteFile.txt','a') as f:
    f.write("more new stuf")


#SECTION8
#let us do another append to the file, this time
    #we will append data on a new line
with open('testWriteFile.txt','a') as f:
    f.write("\nmore new stuff")
```

#END OF PROGRAM

PYTHON SHELL
>>> ===================== RESTART =====================
>>>
Enter your name: Herb
Hi Herb
This is entire file using a simple open
First, Second, Third, John, Fred

first line of lineTextfile
First

the second line of lineTextfile= Second

This is SECTION4 data from simpleTextfile using 'with open'
First, Second, Third, John, Fred

This is SECTION5 data from lineTextfile using 'with open'
First

Second

Third

John

Fred

This is SECTION6 data from lineTextfile with automatic line feed off
First
Second
Third
John
Fred

ERROR HANDLING

Python has some very nice error handling features. Sometimes the procedure is called 'try or throw and catch' or more formally as 'try' and 'except'. Files are a good place to continue with intentionally generating some errors and handling them.

In our next program 'errorTrapping.py' I have set up for two files to be opened. The first file does not exist. The second file does exist, from our prior session. When you try to run the program it blows up when it cannot find the file with an IOError and never reaches the second file opening.

errorTrapping.py   error generation no trapping

```
# errorTrapping.py   error generation no trapping
```

```
#START PROGRAM
# using Python3.2.2
# author Herb  8/2/2013 RyMax, Inc.


#open file which does not exist
fileName="noSuchFile"
f= open(fileName,'r')



# open file which exists
print ('ready to open second file')
fileName="lineTextfile.txt"
f= open(fileName,'r')


#END OF PROGRAM
```

PYTHON SHELL
```
>>> ===================== RESTART =====================
>>>
Traceback (most recent call last):
  File "C:\Documents and Settings\All Users\Documents\BOOKexhibits\Python32\errorTrapping.py", line 8, in <module>
    f= open(fileName,'r')
IOError: [Errno 2] No such file or directory: 'noSuchFile'
>>>
```

We need our program to handle the error and give the operator information, and most of all keep the program running. I am going to start with a simple Try and Except routine. Notice the indents and the colons following try and except statements.

errorTrappingTRY.py   error trapping and methods to handle

```
#START PROGRAM
# using Python3.2.2
# author Herb  8/2/2013 RyMax, Inc.

#try to open file which does not exist
try:
    fileName="noSuchFile"
    f= open(fileName,'r')
except:
    print ("Program error could not open file named= ",fileName)

#try to open file which exists
print ('ready to open second file')
fileName="lineTextfile.txt"
f= open(fileName,'r')
#END OF PROGRAM
```

PYTHON SHELL
```
>>> ===================== RESTART =====================
>>>
Program error could not open file named=  noSuchFile
```

ready to open second file
>>>

While the program kept running and did inform us of an error it really is not giving a lot of information. We can refine the error handling process. Let's also give the user the chance to correct the error and continue running the program.

In the next program the error handling is improved and the user is given a chance to correct the error. If the error is not corrected the program will cleanly exit. For this exit to process we need to import the module 'os'. If you leave out the last 'os.exit(0)' shown in the code as the last statement you can get some interesting results. What can happen is that the variable names are not cleared as the program may not have stopped running. It is a good idea to make sure your program has stopped running. I think this is something within the IDLE programs that can cause this. I do not ever recall having a similar problem when running from a command prompt. There are many levels of refinement that can be achieved; this example hopefully gives you a good start.

 # errorTrappingImproved.py   error trapping and methods to handle

```
#START PROGRAM
# using Python3.2.2
# author Herb  8/2/2013 RyMax, Inc.

import os      #need this for exit to work

#try to open file which does not exist
try:
   fileName="noSuchFile"
   f= open(fileName,'r')
except IOError as err:
   print ("read Error Code:= ", err)
   #another way of formatting the error message
   print ("Error Description: {0}".format(err))
   #ask user if they would like to enter filename
   try:
      newResponse=int(input("Enter 1 to Continue, 0 to Exit "))
   except:   # ValueError:
      print ("not a valid input program will end")
      os._exit(1)
   #if response is a number 1
      #GIVE THE USER A CHANCE TO ENTER FILE
   if (newResponse==1):                #note two = signs
      fileName=input("Enter filename ")
      try:
         f=open(fileName,'r')
         print ("success USER INPUT opening filename= "+fileName)
      except IOError as err:
         print ("Error on user entered filename", fileName)
         print ("Error Description: {0}".format(err))
         print ("not a valid filename program will end")
         os._exit(1)
```

```
    else:
        os._exit(0)

#try to open file which exists
print ('ready to open second file')
fileName="lineTextfile.txt"
try:
    f= open(fileName,'r')
    print ("second file successfully opened filename= "+fileName)
except IOError as err:
    print ("Error on user entered filename")
    print ("Error Description: {0}".format(err))
    print ("not a valid filename program will end")
    os._exit(1)
os._exit(0)
#END OF PROGRAM
```

```
PYTHON SHELL  (Note when I ran it I entered at the prompt a number 1, then the filename    lineTextfile.txt
>>> ======================= RESTART =======================
>>>
read Error Code:= [Errno 2] No such file or directory: 'noSuchFile'
Error Description: [Errno 2] No such file or directory: 'noSuchFile'
Enter 1 to Continue, 0 to Exit 1
Enter filename lineTextfile.txt
success USER INPUT opening filename= lineTextfile.txt
ready to open second file
second file successfully opened filename= lineTextfile.txt

>>> ======================= RESTART =======================
>>>
```

LOOPING

We have all these great tools, but to get to the real power of computing we need to be able to loop through events. One simple method is by using a 'for' loop. In this method we set a range and the program executes all the indented items under the 'for' statement.

The second method involves having a group of statements that are indented under a 'while' statement. You may recall our bool examples. In our example we in effect say 'while the counter value is true keep executing the loop'. Remember 'True' is just about any value other than 0.

looping.py   Keeping the program running

```
#START PROGRAM
#START PORGRAM
# using Python3.2.2
# author Herb  8/2/2013 RyMax, Inc.

for x in range(0,5):  #one of the simplest looping concepts is the 'for' loop
        print ("x is = ",x)
print()
print ("when x = 3 we want to exit the loop")
for x in range(0,5):
```

```
          print ("x is = ",x)
          if (x == 3):
                    break
print ()
print ("countdown")
y=6
for x in range(0,5):
          y-=1
          print ("y is = ",y)
print ("Blastoff")
print ()
print ("run  while True")
print ("would run forever, but we stop at 10, set counter=0, becomes False and ends loop")
counter = 1
while counter:              #as long as counter not = to 0 will run
          counter+=1
          print (counter)
          if counter ==10:
                    counter=0
#END OF PROGRAM
```

PYTHON SHELL
>>> ===================== RESTART =====================
>>>
x is = 0
x is = 1
x is = 2
x is = 3
x is = 4

when x = 3 we want to exit the loop
x is = 0
x is = 1
x is = 2
x is = 3

countdown
y is = 5
y is = 4
y is = 3
y is = 2
y is = 1
Blastoff

run while True
would run forever, but we stop at 10, set counter=0, becomes False and ends loop
2
3
4
5
6
7
8
9
10

```
>>>
```

Infinite Loop

What if we want our program to run until we tell it to stop?   Then we need to setup a while loop that stays true until the user tells it to stop. Of course if in a loop how do we have the user stop the program? One method is to use Ctrl + C.   This is what I would call a 'hard stop' really a last resort for exiting the program. But give it a try then we can refine it. Note for Linux-Debian users, if you cannot stop the program you can look up the PID from a terminal prompt by typing 'top', look for the idle process and note the PID number. Then stop the 'top' process by typing Ctrl + z, or from another terminal prompt enter 'kill PID#'.

 # infiniteLoop.py   Keeping the program running forever

```
#START PROGRAM
# infiniteLoop.py   Keeping the program running forever
# using Python3.2.2
# author Herb  8/2/2013 RyMax, Inc.

print (' Program is running, to stop press Ctrl + c key')
while True:
    print ('Hi')

#END OF PROGRAM

PYTHON SHELL
>>>> ====================== RESTART ======================
>>>
 Program is running, to stop press Ctrl + c key
Hi
Hi
Hi
Hi
Hi
Traceback (most recent call last):
  File "C:\Documents and Settings\All Users\Documents\BOOKexhibits\Python32\infiniteLoop.py", line 8, in <module>
    print ('Hi')
KeyboardInterrupt
>>>
```

Well it did stop, not pretty, but it stopped. In the next program we are going to ask the user to enter values using our 'raw_input'. We will test the input. First we need to remember that Python is treating our input as a string, so we need to convert it to an integer. Then, if the conversion is successful we test the integer value to see if it is the integer 99. If that is true we set our while statement to False. The False value ends the 'while loop' and the program ends. I left the Ctrl C message in just in case so you would remember how to stop a runaway train. You will also see in our 'except:' statement that we have the action defined as 'pass'. You can think of 'pass' as a place holder or empty statement that means just as you would think, go ahead and do nothing.

 # infiniteLoopDataEntry.py   Keeping the program running until user stops it

```
#START PROGRAM
# using Python3.2.2
# author Herb  8/2/2013 RyMax, Inc.
```

```
print (' Program is running, to stop press Ctrl + c key if all else fails')
runValue=True
userNumber=0

while runValue:
    userValue=input("Enter 99 to stop program  ")
    print ('user entered: '+userValue)

    try:
        userNumber = int(userValue)
        if userNumber==99:
            runValue=False
            print ('program stop value entered')
    except:
        pass          #no action

#END OF PROGRAM
```

PYTHON SHELL
```
>>> ===================== RESTART ======================
>>>
 Program is running, to stop press Ctrl + c key if all else fails
Enter 99 to stop program  my name is Herb
user entered: my name is Herb
Enter 99 to stop program  88
user entered: 88
Enter 99 to stop program  99
user entered: 99
program stop value entered
>>>
```

USER DEFINED FUNCTIONS

As our programs become more complicated we will want to separate activities into separate areas. This will help a reader of the program figure out what is going on and greatly help us debug the program. That is in the unlikely event that we make an error, ha.

Let's take the program we just completed and setup our input prompt in a function. A function or procedure or call routine is just a block of code that is called or run from another section of code. Python treats the variables within a function as independent to that function. For example in our code from above the variable 'runValue' within the function is a completely independent variable from the variable defined outside the function. There are several ways to 'tie' the variable to the function. The first way we will explore is the 'global' definition.

With global definitions you must define the variable as global prior to changing the value of the variable. As we are going to change the variable's value within our function we must declare it as global within the function and prior to making the change.

function.py   Organizing our code in functions

```
#START PROGRAM
# using Python3.2.2
# author Herb  8/3/2013 RyMax, Inc.
```

```
print (' Program is running, to stop press Ctrl + c key if all else fails')
global runValue
runValue=True

def userInputFunction():
    global runValue
    userValue=input("Enter 99 to stop program  ")
    print ('user entered: '+userValue)

    try:
        userNumber=0
        userNumber = int(userValue)
        if userNumber==99:
            runValue=False
            print ('program stop value entered')
    except:
        pass           #no action

while runValue:
    userInputFunction()
    print ("In while loop runValue= ", end="")
    print (runValue)

#END OF PROGRAM
PYTHON SHELL
>>> ====================== RESTART ======================
>>>
 Program is running, to stop press Ctrl + c key if all else fails
Enter 99 to stop program  keep running
user entered: keep running
In while loop runValue= True
Enter 99 to stop program  99
user entered: 99
program stop value entered
In while loop runValue= False
>>>
```

In the function shown above we are not passing variable's to or from the function. Let us rework our example and actually pass the variable to the function. In the following we walk through the actions occurring. First we define runValue as True. Then in our while loop we call our function. Note within the ( ) we have put our variable, and that variable is received within our defined function, as a variable named runValueRec. I then moved the value to our runValue variable and did the tests as before. At the end of the function we have added a return(runValue). This passes the variable runValue back to the statement that called the function. At that point I assigned the value to the variable runValueReturned. I then moved the value to our runValue to continue on with the program. I put the extra steps into help show which variable is being passed and returned. In the following programs I show one program with the extra steps and one simplified.

You can pass multiple variables to a function. You just need to have the same number of arguments in the receiving and the calling statements.

functionPassVariable.py   Organizing our code in functions

```
#START PROGRAM
# using Python3.2.2
```

```
# author Herb  8/2/2013 RyMax, Inc.

print (' Program is running, to stop press Ctrl + c key if all else fails')
runValue=True

def userInputFunction(runValueRec):
   runValue=runValueRec
   userValue=input("Enter 99 to stop program  ")
   print ('user entered: '+userValue)

   try:
      userNumber=0
      userNumber = int(userValue)
      if userNumber==99:
         runValue=False
         print ('program stop value entered')
   except:
      pass            #no action
   return(runValue)

while runValue:            #as long as runValue is true program will run
   runValueReturned=userInputFunction(runValue)
   runValue=runValueReturned
   print ("In while loop runValue= ",end="")
   print (runValue)

#END OF PROGRAM
```

PYTHON SHELL
```
>>> ===================== RESTART =====================
>>>
 Program is running, to stop press Ctrl + c key if all else fails
Enter 99 to stop program  no
user entered: no
In while loop runValue=  True
Enter 99 to stop program  99
user entered: 99
program stop value entered
In while loop runValue=  False
>>>
```

The following is the simpler version for passing variables to and from functions.

functionPassVariable2.py   *Organizing our code in functions*

```
 #START PROGRAM
# using Python3.2.2
# author Herb  8/2/2013 RyMax, Inc.

print (' Program is running, to stop press Ctrl + c key if all else fails')
runValue=True
```

```python
def userInputFunction(runValue):
    userValue=input("Enter 99 to stop program  ")
    print ('user entered: '+userValue)

    try:
        userNumber=0
        userNumber = int(userValue)
        if userNumber==99:
            runValue=False
            print ('program stop value entered')
    except:
        pass          #no action
    return(runValue)

while runValue:          #as long as runValue is true program will run
    runValue=userInputFunction(runValue)
    print ("In while loop runValue= ",end="")
    print (runValue)
```

#END OF PROGRAM

PYTHON SHELL
```
>>> ===================== RESTART =====================
>>>
 Program is running, to stop press Ctrl + c key if all else fails
Enter 99 to stop program  fsdgfsdg
user entered: fsdgfsdg
In while loop runValue=  True
Enter 99 to stop program  99
user entered: 99
program stop value entered
In while loop runValue=  False
>>>
```

Classes

Another method you will want to know as your programs become more complicated involves the use of 'CLASSES'. We are going to do a very simple program using 'CLASS'. This program will from the user perspective work just as our previous program. Our first step is to define our 'CLASS', much like the design of a house. We give the CLASS or design a name, here I called it 'ourFirstClass', note we end the line with a colon. We then need to define and initialize our class. Remember to indent, IDLE does a decent job of setting this up for you. In our init statement note there are two underscores on either end of 'init'. Then in brackets we first give our class a structure. The first item has to be the data name and then the attributes of the data follow separated by a comma. We close with brackets and add a colon. Then on the next line, which is indented, enter the variables that are going to be used to define our initial values for the data. Then assign initial values to our class variables. Now this is a lot of work for just one variable, but when you have a number of them it becomes very useful. As you can see the data elements are somewhat global in nature.

class.py   Organizing our code CLASS and functions

#START PROGRAM
using Python3.2.2
author Herb 8/3/2013 RyMax, Inc.

```
print (' Program is running, to stop press Ctrl + c key if all else fails')

class ourFirstClass:
    def __init__(OurData, runValue):
        OurData.runValue=runValue

myDataAssign=ourFirstClass(
    runValue=True)


def userInputFunction():
    userValue=input("Enter 99 to stop program  ")
    print ('user entered: '+userValue)

    try:
        userNumber=0
        userNumber = int(userValue)
        if userNumber==99:
            myDataAssign.runValue=False
            print ('program stop value entered')
    except:
        pass            #no action
    return()

while myDataAssign.runValue:            #as long as runValue is true program will run
    userInputFunction()
    print ("In while loop runValue= ",end="")
    print (myDataAssign.runValue)

#END OF PROGRAM

PYTHON SHELL
>>> ====================== RESTART ======================
>>>
 Program is running, to stop press Ctrl + c key if all else fails
Enter 99 to stop program  hhhh
user entered: hhhh
In while loop runValue= True
Enter 99 to stop program  adsa
user entered: adsa
In while loop runValue= True
Enter 99 to stop program  88
user entered: 88
In while loop runValue= True
Enter 99 to stop program  99
user entered: 99
program stop value entered
In while loop runValue= False
>>>
```

LIST DATA TYPE

Python also provides some other very useful methods for handling data. The next one we will look at is the list data type. Think of the list as a stack of books. To get to a book you need to move down the stack and find the book that you want. You can also refer to the fourth item or book in the stack, you can sort the stack of books, remove books and of course add books, to name a few actions.

You define your list by putting the values in [ ] with each value separated by a comma. If you have a string you need to enclose in quotations, either single or double.

Once the 'list' is defined you can use the existing methods of the 'list' data type to make changes to the list. The following program demonstrates many of the list methods.

list.py   Understanding the List Data Type

```
#START PROGRAM
# using Python3.2.2
# author Herb  8/3/2013 RyMax, Inc.

#define a list
myList = ['John', 'Bill', 'Henry','88', 'John','John','22']
print (myList)

#how many times does the name 'John' appear in the list
print ("the name 'John' occurs ",end="")
print (myList.count('John'),end="")
print (" times in my List")

#print (the fourth item in the list, note list index starts at zero
print ('the fourth item in my list is ',end="")
print (myList[3])

print ('My sorted list ')
myList.sort()
print (myList)

#if I want to find the index of a value in the list
myIndex= myList.index('Bill')
print ("'Bill' is in index postion ", myIndex)

print ("I want to now remove 'Bill' from my list")
myList.pop(2)
print (myList)

print ("I want to insert 'Tom' at index postion 2")
myList.insert(2,"Tom")
print (myList)

print ("I want to append 'Jenny' to the end of the list")
myList.append("Jenny")
print (myList)

#END OF PROGRAM

PYTHON SHELL
>>> ====================== RESTART ======================
>>>
```

['John', 'Bill', 'Henry', '88', 'John', 'John', '22']
the name 'John' occurs 3 times in my List
the fourth item in my list is 88
My sorted list
['22', '88', 'Bill', 'Henry', 'John', 'John', 'John']
'Bill' is in index postion 2
I want to now remove 'Bill' from my list
['22', '88', 'Henry', 'John', 'John', 'John']
I want to insert 'Tom' at index postion 2
['22', '88', 'Tom', 'Henry', 'John', 'John', 'John']
I want to append 'Jenny' to the end of the list
['22', '88', 'Tom', 'Henry', 'John', 'John', 'John', 'Jenny']
>>>

LIST Writing and Reading from file

We should consider how to write a list to a file and of course how to read the file back into a list. Python provides a lot of very useful tools for these purposes.   We will write our list to a 'txt' file and then read the 'txt' file back into a separate list. When you write to a file you will want to have a delimiter, many times a comma is used in text files. For this test I am adding a line feed. If you look at the file we create in the editor you will see it is very readable. When we read the file back in we want to eliminate the line feed. Python has very nice tools for handling these actions as you will see in the following program.

 # listFile.py   Writing and reading List to/from file

```
#START PROGRAM
# using Python3.2.2
# author Herb  8/3/2013 RyMax, Inc.

#define a list needs to be all strings
myList = ['John', 'Bill', 'Henry','88', 'John','John','22']
print (myList)
fileName='listFile.txt'
try:
    f= open(fileName,'w')
    print ("File opened ", fileName)
except IOError as err:
    print ("read Error Code:= ", err)

try:
    for item in myList:
        f.write(item)
        f.write("\n")
        print ('item written')
except IOError as err:
    print ("read Error Code:= ", err)

f.close()

#open listFile.txt just written to, and read into newList
#in writing the file I added a new line control which you probably
#will want to strip from the data.  Using a string method 'strip'
```

```
try:
    with open(fileName) as f:
        newList =[line.strip() for line in f]
except IOError as err:
    print ("read Error Code:= ", err)


print ('This is the newList' )
print (newList)
print ('Item five in the list is: ',newList[4])
#END OF PROGRAM
```

PYTHON SHELL
```
>>> ===================== RESTART =====================
>>>
['John', 'Bill', 'Henry', '88', 'John', 'John', '22']
File opened  listFile.txt
item written
item written
item written
item written
item written
item written
item written
This is the newList
['John', 'Bill', 'Henry', '88', 'John', 'John', '22']
Item five in the list is:  John
>>>
```

ARRAY MODULE

Arrays are similar to List Data Types but are constrained to one data type per array.   Try to add a string to the array defined below, you will get an error. The Array Data Types that can be defined are shown in the following table.

Type Code	Python Type
'c'	character
'b'	int
'B'	int
'u'	Unicode character
'h'	int
'H'	int
'i'	int
'I'	long
'l'	int
'L'	long
'f'	float
'd'	float

Many of the Type Codes are defined as 'int' or integer in Python. This is due to the close relationships between 'C' language and Python. One of the many nice features of arrays is that you are setting up a

'CLASS' when you define an array that is available somewhat globally.   In our next program I defined an integer array. To prove it is available in a function, I print the array from a function. Note the difference in usage between ( ) and [ ]. Consider the ( ) for function and the [ ] for index values.

array.py   Understanding the Array Data Type

```
#START PROGRAM
# using Python3.2.2
# author Herb  8/4/2013 RyMax, Inc.

import array

#define an array consisting of unsigned integers
myUnsignedIntegerArray=array.array('i', [22,33,12,15,25,100,12000])
print ( myUnsignedIntegerArray)

#find first occurance of 12 and print ( the index
whereIsIt=myUnsignedIntegerArray.index(12)
print ( 'The number 12 is located in index postion ', whereIsIt)
print ( "The value of index 2 is ", myUnsignedIntegerArray[2])
#remove the first occurance of 15
myUnsignedIntegerArray.remove(15)
print ( myUnsignedIntegerArray)

def testFunction():
    print ( 'at test function ', myUnsignedIntegerArray)
count=1
runTime=True
print ( "Remember Ctrl + C key to stop run away train if you need it")
while runTime:
    testFunction()
    count=count+1
    if (count>1):
        runTime=False

#END OF PROGRAM

PYTHON SHELL
>>> ===================== RESTART =====================
>>>
array('i', [22, 33, 12, 15, 25, 100, 12000])
The number 12 is located in index position  2
The value of index 2 is  12
array('i', [22, 33, 12, 25, 100, 12000])
Remember Ctrl + C key to stop run away train if you need it
at test function  array('i', [22, 33, 12, 25, 100, 12000])
>>>
```

ARRAY WRITE AND READ FILE

Before we leave arrays, let us have our program write the array data to a file. This gets a little confusing, but I think some of the confusion occurs due to what happens in the background as you run the various methods. See the following example where we write an integer array to a txt file using the binary write and then read the file back in to a different array, using a binary read. Note how the integers are converted to binary and written to the file without you taking any action.

arrayFile.py Array files writing and reading

```python
#START PROGRAM
# using Python3.2.2
# author Herb  8/4/2013 RyMax, Inc.

import array
import sys

#define an array consisting of unsigned integers
myIntegerArray=array.array('l', [22,33,12,15,25,100,12000])
print (myIntegerArray)
myArrayType=myIntegerArray.typecode
print ("Array type code is: ",myArrayType)
print ('This is data item 4 of myIntegerArray ',myIntegerArray[3])
#append some integers to the array
myIntegerArray.append(109)
myIntegerArray.append(410)
print ('After appending ',myIntegerArray)

#we do not need to convert the integer array to a string array
#using something like  myIntegerArray.tostring()
#when we write using .tofile the array is converted to machine values

#write the array to a file note uses machine values
fileName='myArrayFile.txt'
try:
    f= open(fileName,'wb')
    print ( "File opened for write ", fileName)
    myIntegerArray.tofile(f)
except IOError as err:
    print ( "read Error Code:= ", err)
f.close()

#open file and read into different array name
try:
    f= open(fileName,'rb')
    print ( "File opened for read ", fileName)
    #define a new array
    newArray=array.array('i',[])
    newArray.fromfile(f,50)
except IOError as err:
    print ( "read Error Code:= ", err)
except:
    pass
#in reading from array using fromfile, set number of items
#for more than in file, will generate error if not enought
#items in file so use the try and except method

print ('this is the newArray file data')
```

```
print (newArray)

#see what data type Python thinks the newArray is
arrayType = type(newArray)
print (arrayType)
myArrayType=myIntegerArray.typecode
print ("Array type code is: ",myArrayType)
#print ( data item 4 which is index item 3 of our new file
print ('This is data item 4 of newArray ',newArray[3])

#END OF PROGRAM

PYTHON SHELL
>>> ===================== RESTART =====================
>>>
array('l', [22, 33, 12, 15, 25, 100, 12000])
Array type code is:  l
This is data item 4 of myIntegerArray  15
After appending  array('l', [22, 33, 12, 15, 25, 100, 12000, 109, 410])
File opened for write  myArrayFile.txt
File opened for read  myArrayFile.txt
this is the newArray file data
array('i', [22, 33, 12, 15, 25, 100, 12000, 109, 410])
<class 'array.array'>
Array type code is:  l
This is data item 4 of newArray  15
>>>
```

ARRAY READ AND WRITE USING PICKLE

In our previous example you could see that the text editor was useless in reading the file. Another feature of Python for working with arrays is the 'pickle' module. This is a method of serializing and de-serializing the Python object. You can use the editor to look at the file generated and I do recommend that you take a look. You can recognize your values if you look closely. The following is a quick view to give you the flavor of the process.

 # arrayFilePickle.py   Array's using Pickle

```
#START PROGRAM
# using Python3.2.2
# author Herb  8/4/2013 RyMax, Inc.

import array
import pickle
import sys

#define an array consisting of unsigned integers
myUnsignedIntegerArray=array.array('i', [22,33,12,15,25,100,12000])
print ( myUnsignedIntegerArray)

#append some integers to the array
myUnsignedIntegerArray.append(109)
myUnsignedIntegerArray.append(410)
```

```python
print ( myUnsignedIntegerArray)

#write the array to a file
fileName='myPickleFile.pk1'
try:
   f= open(fileName,'wb')
   print ( "File opened ", fileName)
except IOError as err:
   print ( "read Error Code:= ", err)
except:
   print ( "General Error: ")

pickle.dump(myUnsignedIntegerArray, f,0)
f.close()

#open file and read into different array name
try:
   f= open(fileName,'rb')
   print ( "File opened ", fileName)
except IOError as err:
   print ( "Open Error: ", err)

newArray=array.array('i',[])
newArray=pickle.load(f)
print ( 'this is the new array file')
print ( newArray)
f.close()
# print ( item 3 of array
print ( "Item 3 of array has a value of ",newArray[2])

#see what data type Python thinks the newArray is
arrayType = type(newArray)
print ( arrayType)
myArrayType=newArray.typecode
print ("Array type code is: ",myArrayType)

#END OF PROGRAM
```

PYTHON SHELL
```
>>> ===================== RESTART =====================
>>>
array('i', [22, 33, 12, 15, 25, 100, 12000])
array('i', [22, 33, 12, 15, 25, 100, 12000, 109, 410])
File opened  myPickleFile.pk1
File opened  myPickleFile.pk1
this is the new array file
array('i', [22, 33, 12, 15, 25, 100, 12000, 109, 410])
Item 3 of array has a value of  12
<class 'array.array'>
Array type code is:  i
>>>
```

The data file 'myPickleFile.pk1 has the output shown in the following.
carray
array
p0
(Vi
p1
(lp2
L22L
aL33L
aL12L
aL15L
aL25L
aL100L
aL12000L
aL109L
aL410L
atp3
Rp4
.

OTHER EDITORS
As you have seen IDLE is nice, but it has shortcomings. As your programs grow larger it is very nice to have line numbers displayed by the editor. There may be other problems that you encounter so it would be nice to have some choices. I have found two that I like. The 'Programmer's Notepad' is very nice, but I do not think it is available for Linux. For Windows users it is a great choice. For Linux users I like 'Geany' as well as the standard 'vim' or 'vi'. Geany is available for Windows and Linux. I have included some information for obtaining and installing these editors. There are many other options for editors. Don't forget to give PythonWin a chance if you are running Windows. Before you give up on IDLE you may want to consider some of the extensions that are available. One example is IDLEX, you can check it out at:
    http://idlex.sourceforge.net/screenshots.html .

Programmer's Notepad

If you are going to need some additional tools later, specifically a C compiler with libraries, I suggest you look at this one. Go to http://winavr.sourceforge.net/download.html. Select download and follow the instructions. The version I am currently using is WinAvr-2010 and is approximately 28.8Mb. The editor is called Programmer's Notepad.

Geany For Windows

The program has many useful features. Go to www.geany.org I have the geany-1.2.3.1 setup.exe Full Installer, approximately 8Mb. This has some nice features for configuration of makeFile if you are going to need to compile programs other than Python. While it supports what you need for Python I would not say it was designed for Python, but I have found it to work well with Python.

Geany For Linux-Debian

Available under Synaptic Package Manager. Also under aptitude and apt-get install geany.

Simple DOS commands
For those who may have forgotten some simple DOS commands, a very quick refresher course follows. I am going to create a directory in the location where my 'cmd' prompt opened. Adjust the following as needed

for your system.   Before we go any further, a few quick words on DOS commands. They can do damage, they are not very user friendly; they will destroy without asking twice. So make sure the command you enter is the command that you want and that you know what the command is going to do.

Simple DOS commands, execute from the DOS command prompt. Remember DOS is not case sensitive.

- Dir or dir   – This will give you the contents of the current directory
- Help   – all the commands that are available
- Help dir   – gives you all the options available with dir
- cd {dir name}– change directory, you would add the directory name
- cd ../   – moves up the directory tree one level
- cls   –clear the DOS window screen

To create a directory to store our programs. Call the directory 'work'.

mkdir work   –this will create the directory

To see if the directory was created type 'dir w*' this should list your work directory and any other file or directory starting with 'w' the * is called a wild card.

If you do make the change to another editor be aware that Python needs to be in your system path. When you are using IDLE that is automatically taken care of. On Windows to check if Python is in your path go to the command prompt and type 'path'. You should see the path to your Python directories included. If you do not see it you can add it by typing the following command as modified for your system. For example Path= %path%;c:\python32.   While you can add as an environmental attribute I prefer to put the command in a batch file that I execute each time. If you are using another editor, you may want to run the programs from a dos prompt. To run a program you would type 'python hello.py' for example.

Some Other Python Modules

The Python documentation available under the 'HELP' menu is very useful. Consider the 'Global Module Index', this provides a complete list of all modules available under the version of Python you are running. Modules that are limited to certain operating systems are noted. Also Modules that are 'Depreciated' or being phased out are noted. While you can still use 'Depreciated' modules it is not recommended as in future versions they will probably not be supported. There are too many for me to list, explore them as there are fantastic features. Some of the ones that I frequently use are shown in the following.

'tkinter' - The standard GUI interface, it has a lot features and is extremely useful when writing programs for users that like a window type environment.

threading – As your programs become more sophisticated and you do not want the program to wait until a separate process finishes. I find this very useful in my programs that use serial communication.

time – Very useful for working with any type of time in your programs. I find that with today's processors being as fast as they are that building in slight sleep or delay periods can be desirable.

csv – Another common import and export format for spreadsheets and other databases that use 'Comma Separated Values'.

os – Use this module for working with operating system information, great way to check the operating system name or environment

queue – Very nice and powerful, you can setup multiple queue with priorities, sizes and control the order items are selected in. This can be very useful in communications.

socket – If you are communicating via the internet you will want to work with this module.

subprocess – At some point you will want to load another program while your current one is running. Maybe off a menu, this module allows you to spawn a new process.

sys – Allows you to access variables used by the interpreter, for example the sys.version we used earlier in the book.

There are some modules that are not part of the standard Python releases. For example, if you want to use serial communication a special module must be installed. Do your research on the sites mentioned earlier for obtaining Python. There are a lot of special modules and as you get more involved I am sure you will need some of them for your projects. A few of the ones I have been using include.

serial - Named pyserial if you are looking for it. If you want to use serial communication this is I would think is a must module.

pygame – A nice module for developing games, while you can use Tkinter for a lot of developing GUI, this module can assist you in getting the process going.

pywin32 – If you are working on Windows you will want to get the Windows Extensions for Python. I believe the ActiveState Community version includes this set, or at least part of it.

The End or the Beginning

I hope that you have learned a lot and had some fun. You can continue on to great depth with Python. One of my reasons for learning Python was to control remote process's, such as controlling a robot from my PC. In my book "Robot Wireless Control Made Simple with Python and C" I cover many other Python topics. For example: GUI-tkinter, playing sounds, text to speech, queues, threading, subprocess and serial communication. The book also covers programming microchips with C and the wiring schematics for motors, communications and the H-Bridge.

Visit the web site www.rymax.biz for additional information. I would like to learn from your experience, you can e-mail me at herb@rymax.biz.